GOLDEN TREASURES

Written By
Evangelist Mildred Elizabeth Jenkins

A Part of
The Drea Series
By
Andrea B. Jenkins

Golden Treasures

Written By
Evangelist Mildred Elizabeth Jenkins

A Part of
The Drea Series
By
Andrea B. Jenkins

About the Author

Evangelist Mildred Elizabeth Layne Jenkins was born and educated in Cambridge Massachusetts, at a young age she began writing poetry, prose and inspirational letters

Over the years Evang Jenkins spent more and more time writing which became one of her great loves and was blessed to share her talents with many.

Evangelist. Jenkins' writing was 100% God inspired which prompted her to begin writing under the pen name Elizabeth which means "God is my Oath, Pledged to God and God is my Abundance"

On October 22, 2009, two days after celebrating 53 years of marriage to the love of her life Eld. Ronald A. Jenkins, in His wisdom, God called her back to Himself, back to the origin of where her gift was given.

It was her desire to see this collection of writing published so she could share them with many far and wide, so in her honor, her daughters Andrea and Tara have been blessed with the honor of making her dream a reality.

It is our prayer that as you read each passage, that you will be blessed and encouraged and that in reading you will celebrate the life of this mighty woman of God whose words will continue to penetrate the atmosphere.

Evangelist Mildred Elizabeth Layne Jenkins

January 31, 1935 - October 22, 2009

Submitted in Love By
Daughters
Andrea Jenkins
and
Tara (Jenkins) Johnson

Our Special Rose

God took a walk on a Wednesday and saw a rose so fair,
a rose that shed the light of His love and
wisdom everywhere.

Every petal, individually and collectively, an essence of
strength and peace; so folded in beauty that shall
never cease.

Our Mother, God's choicest rose, fragranced the lives of
those she knew. Patience, Understanding and Kindness,
the bouquet of her radiance and love.

How beautiful He thought, how regal, perfect and pure,
a rose so soft, so fragile and yet the storms edured.

Come with me to a special place, where Roses bloom
fairer than anywhere. He gently picked the tur replica
of handiwork by the Master's Hand, and took the Most
Magnificent Rose to a better land.

This special passage was written in celebration of our
Nana, our mother's dear mother Enid Layne

In turn we take the beautiful words she dedicated to
her own mother and dedicate them to our.

Love You Always Mom

Your Daughters, Andrea & Tara

FLESH OF MY FLESH

YOU ARE FLESH OF MY FLESH AND BONE OF MY BONE, STANDING TOGETHER AS GOD HATH ORDAINED, NEVER AGAIN TO STAND ALONE: UNTIL DEATH CAUSE YOU TO PART.

PLEDGING TO TYPIFY CHRIST'S LOVE FOR HIS CHURCH, FOR YOU'VE BECOME ONE, NO LONGER TWAIN, LOVE OF CHRIST AND LOVE FOR EACH OTHER, WILLINGLY GIVING OF HEART.

HUSBAND HONORING WIFE, WIFE HONORING THE HUSBAND, SUBMISSIVE TO THE FEELINGS AND DESIRES, STEP BY STEP BUILDING A SOLID LIFE, ONE WHICH CAN ONLY TAKE YOUR HIGHER.

CREATED IN GOD'S IMAGE FOR EACH OTHER, TOTALLY COMMITTED TO TENDER CARE, SELFLESS AND THOUGHTFUL…

SHARING JOY AND PAIN,
INSPIRED BY THE LORD WHO BLESSES
SUCH A UNION.

finally

MIX WISDOM & UNDERSTANDING,
HAPPINESS & LAUGHTER, ADD PATIENCE
AND KINDNESS AND ONE IN A WHILE
FLOWERS. BLEND GENTLY WITH GOD'S RAIN
AND THE MILK AND HONEY OF HIS WORD,
THE WINDOWS OF HEAVEN WILL OPEN
SENDING RAYS OF SUNSHINE OF
HIS LOVE… BLESSING WITH
A MARRIAGE SUPREME.

COMMUNION

COMMUNION IS SHARING IN THE SHED
BLOOD OF OUR LORD, THE BODY THAT WAS
BROKEN TO PROVE HIS LOVE, FELLOWSHIP
OF HIS SUFFERING AS TAUGHT IN
THE WORD.

COMMUNION IS REMEMBERING THE
SACRIFICE FOR YOU AND ME, NOT TAKING
FOR GRANTED…THE CROSS OF CALVARY
AND THE GARDEN OF GETHSEMANE.

COMMUNION IS RECEIVING THE CUP
OF BLESSING SO SWEET, THERE'S NO
CONDEMNATION BUT FULL LIBERTY, AS
AROUND THE MASTER'S TABLE WE MEET.

COMMUNION IS PARTAKING OF THE
PRECIOUS BREAD OF LIFE, FREE FROM
BONDAGE AND OPPRESSION
A GIFT OF JESUS CHRIST.

WHAT IS A MOTHER?

Written in Honor of ALL Mothers

A MOTHER IS GOD'S CHOICEST ROSE,
FRAGRACING THE LIVES OF THOSE
SHE KNOWS.

EVERY PETAL, INDIVIDUAL AND
COLLECTIVELY, BLOOMS WITH LOVE
ETERNALLY THE TINY BUD GROWS AND
GROWS UNTIL MATURITY IN GOD'S
KNOWLEDGE FLOWS.

PATIENCE, UNDERSTANDING, KINDNESS
AND WISDOM ARE THE CROWN OF HER
RADIANCE AND LOVE.

WHEREVER AND WHENEVER YOU SEE A
ROSE BLOOM FAIR, YOU'LL KNOW FOR
CERTAIN IT'S A REPLICA OF A
MOTHER THERE!!!

THE BRIDE PREPARES TO MEET HER BRIDEGROOM

SINCE SHE IS A ROYAL PRIESTHOOD, AN HOLY NATION, HER ADORNMENT WILL BE UNLIKE ANY OTHER…

WILL BE WITHOUT SPOT OR WRINKLE OR WITHOUT BLEMISH, OR ANY SUCH THING. SHE WILL BE PRESENTED FAULTLESS ON THAT GREAT DAY WHEN HE SHALL APPEAR TO TAKE HER UNTO HIMSELF WITH EXCEEDING JOY.

SUDDENLY THERE WILL BE A CRY, "BEHOLD THE BRIDEGROOM COMETH." REJOICING GREALY AT HIS VOICE, SHE WILL GO TO MEET HIM.

THEY CRUCIFIED MY LORD

ON A HILL FAR AWAY MANY YEARS AGO
THEY TOOK JESUS TO CALVARY.

IT WAS A LONG AND PAINFUL ORDEAL,
BEGINNING WITH AGONY AT GETHSEMANE.

THE CHIEF PRIESTS AND ELDERS AKK
TOOK COUNSEL TO BEAR FALSE WITNESS
AGAINST HIM.

SINCE THEY WERE NOT SUCCESSFUL, THEY
ACCUSED HIM OF BLASPHEMY AS HE TOLD
THEM OF THE SON OF MAN COMING IN
CLOUDS OF HEAVEN.

RIDICULED, BEATEN, MOCKED, SCOURGED,
LIED UPON AND FOUND GUILTY FOR A
SINNER SUCH AS ME.

HE NEVER MURMURED OR COMPLAINED.
HE HUMBLY HELD HIS PEACE.

ALTHOUGH WITHOUT FAULT, TOOK THE
SHAME FOR HE KNEW SALVATION WE NEED.

THE THORN-CROWNED BROW, THE SPIT,
THE SMOTING REED, AND THE BLOOD
AND WATER THAT STREAMED AS THEY
PIERCED HIS SIDE.

AND GOD SAID

I AM ALPHA AND OMEGA... THE BEGINNING
AND THE END, MY WORD IS TRUTH, ON IT
YOU CAN DEPEND.

I MADE SOMETHING OUT OF NOTHING…
PUT THE SUN, MOON AND STARS IN SPACE.
CREATED IN OUR LIKENESS THE
HUMAN RACE.

I WILL NEVER LEAVE YOU OR FORSAKE
YOU… DO MY WILL. COVENANTED THAT
I WILL BE YOUR GOD AND YOU
MY PEOPLE.

LAY ASIDE EVERY WEIGHT AND WALK BY
FAITH. MY YOKE IS EASY AND MY
BURDEN LIGHT…I AM THE WAY TO
ETERNAL LIFE.

I HAVE NOT TOLD THE ANGELS THE HOUR OF MY APPEARING, BUT BE NOT SLACK NOR SLOTHFUL…THE FINAL MOMENT IS NEARING.

I HAVE LOVED THEE WITH AN EVERLASTING LOVE… IF YOU LOVE ME KEEP MY COMMANDMENTS. OUT OF YOUR BELLY SHALL FLOW RIVERS OF LIVING WATER.

I AM THAT I AM… BESIDE ME THERE IS NO GOD. FOLLOW PEACE WITH ALL E AND REFRAIN FROM SIN, FOR HOLINESS WITHOUT WHICH NO MAN CAN ENTER IN.

FRIENDSHIP

WE WANTED TO BE WITH YOU ON THIS
VERY SPECIAL DAY, SINCE IT WAS NOT
POSSIBLE I AM SENDING THIS
GREETING TO SAY,

WE TREASURE YOUR FRIENDSHIP, IT'S
OF RARE PURE GOLD, MORE BEAUTIFUL
AND PRECIOUS AS IT GROWS OLD.

FOR YEARS YOU HAVE WORKED HARD,
NOW IT'S TIME FOR PLEASURE AND
LEISURE.

MY LOVE AND BEST WISHES ARE YOURS
BEYOND MEASURE,

FULFILLMENT AND HAPPINESS IN
ALL THAT YOU DO,

THESE ARE THE BLESSINGS OUR DEAR
FRIEND WE PRAY FOR YOU.

JOY

JOY IN THE LORD MEANS TO REJOICE;
SINGING MELODIES IN YOUR HEART WITH
A HAPPY VOICE.

THROUGH THE SUNSHINE AND RAIN OR
HEARTACHE AND PAIN; EAT THY BREAD
WITH CONTENTMENT, PROSPERITY
AND GAIN.

KNOW THROUGH FAITH, JOY COMETH IN
THE MORNING; NEW MERCIES,
BLESSINGS AND PEACE WITH
EACH DAWNING.

FATHOM NOT WHEN OR WHY,
DRAW FROM THE WELL'S
BOUNTEOUS SUPPLY.

COUT IT A PRIVILEGE TO LOVE FOR
CHRIST WITH STRENGTH FROM THE
WORD OF GOD.

WHATSOEVER IS LOVELY, PURE AND TRUE;
THINK ON THESE THINGS, AND YOUR LIFE
WILL BE FULL AND NEW.

QUESTION

ARE YOU FAITHFULLY SERVING THE
KING OF LIGHT?

OR

ARE YOU SERVING JOYFULLY THE
KING OF NIGHT?

ARE YOU USING LIBERTY FOR AN
OCCASION TO THE FLESH?

OR

ARE YOU WALKING AND HUNGERING
AFTER GOD'S RIGHTEOUSNESS?

ARE YOUR THOUGHTS AND DESIRES ON
HIGHER GROUND? WILL HE SAY
"WELL DONE?"

OR

DEPART FROM ME YOU INIQUITOUS ONE?

THE PERFECT GIFT

THE ONLY BEGOTTEN SON, WHO CAME
LONG AGO TO ACCOMPLISH THE FATHER;S
PURPOSE FOR THE CREATURES BELOW….
FAITHFUL

THE SEED OF DAVID, THE ROOT OF JESSE,
THE PRECIOUS STONE REJECTED BY THE
BUILDERS, LORD OF LORDS, KING OF
KINGS… THE HEAD CHIEF CORNERSTONE.

A LIFE SACRIFICED BY SHEDDING OF BLOOD,
GIVING ABUNDANT LIFE FOR THE KINGDOM
OF GOD… MAJESTIC

THE LILY OF THE VALLEY, THE WHEEL IN
THE MIDDLE OF THE WHEEL, GIVING JOY,
PEACE, AND BLESSINGS, GOOD TIDINGS
AND LOVE

THE FRUIT OF THE WOMB… <u>HUMAN YET DIVINE</u>. WILL LAST FOREVER, THE BEGINNING AND END OF TIME… <u>IMMUTABLE</u>

THE WONDERFUL COUNSELOR, MIGHTY GOD, THE EVERLASTING FATHER, THE PRINCE OF PEACE WITH RIGHTEOUSNESS AND HEALING IN HIS WINGS.

OMNIPOTENT AND OMNISCIENT, THE WORD, THE SPIRIT, UNQUENCHABLE POWER, BEING IN YOU WITH EVERY HOUR… <u>WITHOUT SPOT OR BLEMISH</u>.

THE GREAT LIGHT MORE PRECIOUS THAN FINE SILVER AND PUREST GOLD, WIDE AND TRUTHFUL, GIRDED ABOUT WITH HOLINESS; CANNOT BE DUPLICATED.

WITHOUT MONEY, WITHOUT PRICE, YOU NEED NOT BUY IT… JESUS CHRIST, THE PROPHESIED SAVIOR. "FOR HE SHALL SAVE HIS PEOPLE FROM THEIR SINS."

MATTHEW 1 - SOLOMON 2:1 - ISAIAH 9:6

WHAT HAVE YOU DONE FOR THE LORD TODAY

WHAT HAVE YOU DONE FOR THE LORD TODAY? DID YOU READ YOUR BIBLE AND REMEMBER TO PRAY? GIVE SOMEONE A SMILE OR LENT AND HELPING HAND? SPOKEN THE RIGHT WORDS SHOWING THE LOVE THAT GOD DEMANDS?

WHAT HAVE YOU DONE FOR THE LORD TODAY? DID YOU TELL SOMEONE ABOUT THE GREAT PLAN OF SALVATION? HOW THE SAVIOR CAME TO SAVE EACH AND EVERY NATION? IS YOUR LIGHT SHINING THAT THE BEAUTY OF JESUS MIGHT BE SEEN? MAKING SOMEONE SAY TO YOU, WHATEVER YOU'VE GOT I NEED?

WHAT HAVE YOU DONE FOR THE LORD TODAY? WALKED IN THE SHOES OF

SOMEONE WHOSE BEEN LESS FORTUNATE THAN YOU? SHOWED COMPASSION AND CONSIDERATION WHEN IT'S EASIER TO BE RUDE? SHARED OR GIVEN WHAT YOU HAVE ALTHOUGH IT MIGHT BE YOUR ALL?

WHAT HAVE YOU DONE FOR THE LORD TODAY? CORRECTED THE ERRORS OF YESTERDAY THROUGH HIS SPIRIT CHANGES YOUR WAYS? THE THORN IN THE FLESH FORGAVE AND ABOVE SELF RISEN? HEARD NO EVIL, SPOKEN NO EVIL, THOUGHT NO EVIL, DID NO EVIL?

WHAT HAVE YOU DONE FOR
THE LORD TODAY?

FORMULA FOR VICTORY

GIVE YOUR BEST… GIVE THE LORD
YOUR ALL.

PRAISE HIM IN ALL THINGS, GREAT
AND SMALL.

PRAY WITHOUT CEASING, WITH
SELF DECREASING.

FAITH WITHOUT FEAR, BELIEF IN THE
LORD INCREASING.

CONFIDENT IN THE LIVING BREAD…
THE WORD.

BE STEADFAST AND WILLING TO SERVE.

OBEDIENT AND HUMBLE AS THE WORD
OF GOD IS HEARD.

STAND STILL SEEING THE SALVATION OF
THE LORD OF HOST.

GLORYING IN HIM WITH A CONTINUAL
DOSE OF THE HOLY GHOST.

FAITH IN GOD

FAITH THAT KNOWS NO WAVERING OR
DEFEAT, COMPLETE VICTORY IT
WILL BRING.

FAITH THAT MADE YOU FIRST BELIEVE AND
THE HOLY GHOST RECEIVE.

FAITH THAT MAKES YOU LIVE THE WORD,
LOVE YOUR ENEMY AS WELL AS GOD.

FAITH THAT HELPS YOU STAND THE TEST,
RESTING IN JESUS SINCE HE KNOWS BEST.

FAITH ENCOURAGES YOU TO SING A
SONG WHEN IT SEEMS ALL HAS
GONE WRONG.

FAITH THAT INCREASES AS SELF DECREASES,
OVERCOMES FLESHLY DESIRES.

FAITH THAT TRUST AND NEVER DOUBTS…
HE IS ABLE TO BRING YOU OUT.

MARK 11:22

AND JESUS ANSWERING SAITH UNTO THEM,
HAVE FAITH IN GOD

GOD IS NOT SLACK

WHAT HE SAYS IN HIS WORD HE WILL DO IT.

HE HAS KEPT YOU THUS FAR TO PROVE IT.

BECAUSE OF HIS LOVE, HE GAVE HIS LIFE TO SHOW IT.

CLOTHED IN THE LILY OF THE FIELD HE'LL PROVIDE YOUR EVERY NEED AND WANTS YOU TO KNOW IT.

THERE IS DEEPNESS IN HIM, POWER IN HIS WORD, SO READ IT.

TRUST GOD AT ALL TIMES, HE NEVER CHANGES, BELIEVE IT.

HIS GIFTS ARE FREE, TO WHOSOEVER BELIEVES, SO ACCEPT IT.

TIMELESS, AGELESS, FAULTLESS, PRICELESS,
ETERNAL EXCELLENCE.

GOD IS NOT SLACK!!

THE BRIDE PREPARES TO MEET HER BRIDEGROOM

THE ENGAGEMENT GIFT HAS BEEN GIVEN… THE HOLY GHOST AND FIRE AND THE PLACE OF THE MARRIAGE IS SET

MUCH TIME IS SPENT IN PREPARATION FOR THAT GREAT DAY. THE SPIRIT WORKING CONSTANTLY TO TAKE ALL IMPERFECTIONS AWAY. HUMILITY, WORSHIP, PRAYER AND PRAISE ARE JUST A FEW OF THE WAYS.

THE COMMUNE DAILY WITH EACH OTHER WITH MUCH LOVE. GOING ABOUT WILLING TO PLEASE HER LOVER… HE IS PUT FIRST, SECOND TO NO OTHER. THE TIME IS AT HAND AND THE UNDERGARMENTS ARE PUT ON… SPIRITUAL ATTIRE. JOY, PEACE, LONGSUFFERING WITH EYES FOR NONE ELES OR WAVERING. GENTLENESS, GOODNESS, MEEKNESS, TEMPERANCE, FAITH AND LOVE, NOT FULLING FLESHLY LUST.

HER GUIDEBOOK BEING THE WORD OF GOD, THE OUTER GARMENTS ARE PUT ON. LOINS ARE GIRDED ABOUT WITH TRUTH, BREASTPLATE OF RIGHTEOUSNESS AND FEED SHOD. HELMET OF SALVATION AND SHIELD OF FAITH… THOSE INGREDIENTS NEEDED TO PATIENTLY WAIT. ALWAYS REPLENISHING HER SUPPLY OF OIL, NOT ALLOWING ANYTHING TO SPOIL

THE GREAT WEDDING

THE GREAT WEDDING IS GOING TO TAKE PLACE, FOR THOSE WHO ARE SAVED AND KEPT BY HIS GRACE. ENOUGH LOVE FOR HIS ENTIRE BRIDE, AS HE GRACIOUSLY AND BEAUTIFULLY USHERS US INSIDE.

THE WEDDING WILL TAKE PLACE IN MID-AIR. ROYALTY AND PRIEST WILL MEET UP THERE. COMING FROM THE NORTH, SOUTH, EAST AND WEST. FOR A MARRIAGE TO A GROOM THAT IS GOD'S BEST.

NO SPOT, WRINKLE, BLEMISH OR ANY SUCH THING. MADE PERFECT AND READY BY THE HEAVENLY KING. A MANSION, A HOME IS ALREADY PREPARED, WITH TWELVE GATES FOR THOSE REVERED. A SPECIAL COURTSHIP NOW COMES TO AN END; WITH A HONEYMOON ETERNAL FOR THE BRIDE AND HER HUSBAND!!